CONTENTS

WINDSCREENS	11
PHILOSOPHY	12
COUNTRY	13
TUXEDO	14
MANTRA	15
TEARS	16
LIBRARY	17
VARIETY	18
RETRIBUTION	20
RABBITS	21
CINEMA	22
DIFFERENCES	24
FENCE	26
FLYING	27
MOON	28
WAG	29
BLUE	30
BLANKED	31
TREE	32
RUT	33
PRIEST	34
GRAVEL	35
ACKNOWLEDGEMENTS	37

© 2024, Vik Shirley. All rights reserved; no part of this book may be reproduced by any means without the publisher's permission.

ISBN: 978-1-916938-65-6

The author has asserted their right to be identified as the author of this Work in accordance with the Copyright, Designs and Patents Act 1988

Cover designed by Aaron Kent

Edited and Typeset by Aaron Kent

Broken Sleep Books Ltd
PO BOX 102
Llandysul
SA44 9BG

PRAISE for *Some Deer*

In Vik Shirley's supremely capable hands language becomes a playground, a laboratory, a lighthouse and a place where surprise becomes the glittering and life-enhancing norm. There are poetic earworms here that will hang around in your mind for a long time.
— Ian McMillan

Deer language, deer politics; their descents into hell (and back); the enigmas and the mayhem. The deer's priest has escaped from a psych ward and isn't really a priest. There's a Nostradamus deer whose warnings go unheeded (country and western music festivals ensue, which have upon the deer a sobering chastity-belt-effect). It's a reality so absurd we recognize it immediately. Equal parts whimsy and menace, Vik Shirley's *Some Deer* is a strange treat.
— Michael Earl Craig

What a relief it is to trample through a world of poems without the problem of people in them. What's left behind is only our pop-culture, or a cardboard cutout of a priest, say, or a hunter, propping up a set for the deer to eek out their own living, joy, and bureaucracies. A whole book like this—just some deer doing deer shit. It would behoove you to read this.
— Zachary Schomburg

I got distracted from quality family time by the marvel of watching Vik Shirley saddle an anaphora to ride across page after page until *Some Deer* became the neon WWJD bracelet I wore through the latest vacuous neoliberal meltdown. In somewhere between a parable and a fable, some deer are studied by rabbits who resort to psychological methods. Vengeance is cinema. Voodoo is jumpsuits. Wrongdoers compete for prize money and the eternal subjectivity of a cave wall drawing. Tail wags instantiate social obligations and aristocratic portraits. Humanity cannot stand to look in the mirror, which is why deer appear to game the scenario. Drippy moon juice, Barry Manilow, and other zine-friendly objects intervene. Inspired by Kristofor Minta's report of deer overpopulating his local Syracuse, these poems don't abscond from the scene of sad rutting. Samuel Beckett created Krapp to think about being and remaining while fixating on the vidua bird and viduity. Agog, quivering like deer at Shirley's disco, I thought again of how absurd we are. And how thrilling to see it so written and ridden.
— Alina Stefanescu

SOME DEER

Vik Shirley is a poet and writer from Bristol now living in Edinburgh. Her books include *Corpses* (Sublunary Editions) and *The Continued Closure of the Blue Door* (HVTN). She has a PhD in Dark Humour and the Surreal in Poetry from the University of Birmingham. Vik co-edits Surreal-Absurd for *Mercurius* and *Firmament* online for Sublunary Editions. Her work has appeared in such places as *Poetry London, PN Review,* and *Dreaming Awake: New and Contemporary Prose Poetry from the United States, Australia and the United Kingdom* (MadHat).

Also by Vik Shirley

Cassette Poems (above/ground, 2024)

One by One (No Press, 2024)

Strangers Wave (zimZalla, 2023)

Notes from the Underworld (Sublunary Editions, 2023)

Poets (The Red Ceilings, 2022)

Grotesquerie for the Apocalypse (Beir Bua Press, 2022)

Disrupted Blue and other poems on Polaroid (Hesterglock, 2021)

The Continued Closure of the Blue Door (HVTN Press, 2021)

Corpses (Sublunary Editions, 2020)

Dedicated to the deer culled in Syracuse, New York, 2023-2024

Some Deer

Vik Shirley

Broken Sleep Books

WINDSCREENS

Some deer ran onto a train track, which soon became an escalator which soon became a descent to hell.
There should be no deer in hell, said someone watching through a crystal-ball-like device, but more modern and Scandinavian in design.
It seemed to be some kind of administrative error, which no one could undo.
So they sent in a swat team, rescued the deer and brought them back into the world.
But the deer weren't really deer afterwards, so affected were they by flashbacks and nightmares.
Woe betide anyone with heated seats who offered them a ride.
Many windscreens were shattered in the Syracuse area.

PHILOSOPHY

Some deer responded to a call.

With trepidation they made their way to the centre of the forest.

A woodland creature, a kind they had never seen before, was stuck in a wire.

It seemed to be ashamed of its pain, something the deer had not encountered before.

What was this shame, they asked each other, in deer language.

It appeared that this poor woodland creature had been spending too much time with humans and their toxic ways.

How very sad for it, the deer agreed in deer language, unaware that at some point during the discussion the creature had died.

COUNTRY

Some deer wanted to frolic, cavort and copulate 24/7.
This was all well and good, said one of the more sensible deer, but they had received a warning from the Nostradamus deer to say that if they did, something bad would happen.
The deer thought the soothsayer was scaremongering and continued to do exactly as they wished.
It was then that a country and western festival started in all deer populated areas.
Everyone knew how much deer had an aversion to country and western music and felt for them, truly, as their cavorting came to a sullen end.

TUXEDO

Some deer lost their appetite and became fussy eaters.
They would only eat oysters and would only drink brandy.
Even then it would all have to be served by a waiter, wearing a tuxedo.
The animal rights folk wanted to help, but it was expensive and hard to get support, given the lavish nature of the deer's requirements.
So they sold the 'waiter' experience to those keen to spend time with deer and in nature and things ran along smoothly until the earth broke apart and swallowed all the waiters into its belly.
Then the deer realised that they were being unreasonable, dropped the tuxedo requirements, and allowed ordinary, leisure-wear clad people to serve them instead.
Please follow the link at the end of this poem if you would like to give it a try.
www.deerwaiterexperienceinleisurewear.org

MANTRA

Some deer planned to go in search of browse, forbs, mast and grass.
They packed some browse, forbs, mast and grass for the journey.
The deer, of which there were four, named, coincidentally, Browse, Forbs, Mast and Grass, practised their meditation, unaware that their guru had given them the exact same mantra, "browse, forbs, mast and grass".
They planned to leave a trail of browse, forbs, mast and grass behind them, in case they got separated or lost.
Also, as part of the preparation, they made a sacrifice to the browse, forbs, mast and grass gods.
By the time they had done all this, they were weary and disturbed after sacrificing one of their young.
They laid down in a circle and disintegrated slowly into the ground.

TEARS

Some deer were chasing their tails.

It was catching, and pretty soon all deer were chasing their tails.

It started a trend and humans began wearing fake deer tails and chasing their tails, too.

Chat shows stopped chatting and instead featured celebrities chasing their tails around the studio.

It was kind of fun, but eventually everyone got dizzy and collapsed.

Then some deer started crying and all the humans started crying too.

The chat shows became just people on the floor crying, until everybody, in the tears, drowned.

LIBRARY

Some deer wanted a library.

Other deer wanted a swimming pool.

The deer who wanted a library thought this was ridiculous, given that there were lakes and streams and so forth.

But the deer who wanted a swimming pool said they weren't hygienic, that they would prefer to have something with chlorine in.

They put up a good argument, but, ultimately, the deer who wanted a library won.

When the library opened, the deer who wanted a swimming pool took out all the books on swimming pools.

It was a poor substitute, but it passed the time until victory would be theirs.

Oh yes, victory would be theirs, they said regularly and knowingly at every opportunity, much to the annoyance of the deer who wanted a library, who really hoped they'd be over this thing by now.

VARIETY

Some deer were tired, so they found a little area to lie down in.
Together they started to dream.
When they were dreaming, they saw each other in their dreams, as had been the case in recent weeks.
This was kind of boring, as they always saw each other when they *weren't* dreaming, and all looked the same.
It would have been nice to see something different in their slumber, they agreed, in deer language.
The deer started to feel bitter, cheated, and, yes, duped, even.
They began to snub each other and do their own thing, making excuses when they headed off solo to do deer shit.
Then one night the Nostradamus deer had a premonition about a big ball of fire coming down from the sky to end the world.
This made them reassess.
They *needed* each other.
So, they clubbed in for plastic surgery for them all, as that way, if they changed their appearances, they could stay together and dream together, but still get the variety they so desperately craved.

Sadly, they didn't check with each other what plastic surgery they were having, and all the deer ended up looking like Andrei Tarkovsky.

It was a change in the short-term at least, they reassured each other, twitching their moustache implants slowly. Very, very slowly.

RETRIBUTION

Some deer walked around in vicious circles and couldn't get out.

The circles were made of barbed wire and snapped at them with venomous teeth (a unique feature of these particular vicious circles).

They also spread awful rumours about the deer, even about the baby ones.

The deer wondered what they had done to deserve getting trapped inside these circles and how they could escape.

It transpired that it had something to do with a slight against an otter back in 1972, during the Great Woodland Crisis, part of the even bigger Forest Landscape Dispute.

The otter appeared at some point, explained that he was now satisfied that "justice had prevailed" and told them all they had to do was say "stop" and the circles would disappear.

Apparently, they could have done this any time in the last 36 months.

RABBITS

A colony of rabbits started to follow some deer.

The deer tried moving, basing themselves in different areas of the forest and so forth, but the rabbits found them wherever they went.

It was as if they were being stalked, they discussed, in deer language.

No one wanted to go down the trap route, but the idea was certainly floated.

They decided instead to out-psych them and try reverse psychology.

If t*hey* started following *them*, perhaps this would stop the cycle.

But the rabbits were ready for them and stood their ground, which resulted in a stand-off that lasted 82 years.

By this time, the animals still living (none), couldn't remember why they were stood there in the first place.

CINEMA

Some deer started to get into cinema.

There was an outdoor cinema on the edge of the forest, and they began going along and watching from the outskirts.

They would save up their browse, forbs, mast and grass for snacks, and turn their phones off during the main feature.

If anyone would make a sound during the movie, they would be hooved, quite aggressively.

Afterwards they would have a conflab about the themes of the movie.

They started to stage plays by the river so that they could glance at their reflections, and it was like watching themselves on screen.

They fell in love with their own reflections, so much so that they *became* their reflections and migrated over fully to reflection form.

The baby deer missed their mummies and daddies who had done this and swore vengeance on cinema.

They dedicated their lives to Vengeance for Parents and listened to radio instead, as a statement.

Occasionally they would wander over to the cinema on the edge of the woods that started this obsession and loiter around the entrance, treating it like a toilet, leaving 'surprises' when people were watching a film so they would encounter their 'nasty packages' when they exited.

It was a small protest, but a potent one, they all agreed, fairly satisfied, in deer language.

DIFFERENCES

Some deer watched listened and learned.
Others just watched and listened.
A few watched, then switched to listening rather than doing all three simultaneously.
All deer publicly said that everyone did things differently, that it was just a matter of taste, that every brain worked uniquely and that all ways were equal.
But secretly, the ones that watched listened and learned simultaneously judged the ones who didn't.
They met at night and wore hoods and capes of dark hues.
They did little spells, using doll replicas of the other deer.
But the other deer soon cottoned on and followed them, surprising and naming and shaming them.
Once cancelled, the deer had to reflect on their actions and knitted the other deer woollen jumpsuits in an array of colours by way of an apology, which went down well and was a significant building block in terms of integrating them back into deer society.
In fact, the jumpsuits caught on with deer in other forests too.

Pretty soon the wrongdoer deer became really successful, and the slighted deer were a bit miffed about the whole thing and wished they'd never given them a second chance.

FENCE

A fence appeared and then disappeared as quickly as it came.

This happened again and again, then it stayed for a day or so before eventually disappearing once more.

Was this some kind of collective hallucination, the deer asked themselves in deer language.

They observed this net-like fence, trying to work out if there was a set pattern.

A few deer lay down over the line where the fence was appearing, and it was as if each had been put in a magician's box, either their front half or back half disappeared.

To confuse things further, a pot of gold appeared at both ends of the fence and some kind of tennis match seemed to be taking place over their heads or rears.

It didn't look like anything was going to be resolved or any questions answered, so the deer decided to take advantage of the strawberries and cream on offer in between games.

What a luxury, they exclaimed to each other in deer language with their mouths full.

The pots of gold were put to use for sponsorship and prize money.

A clubhouse was erected around them, this too flickered in and out of existence, but, luckily for them, the strawberries and cream supplies were more solidly consistent.

FLYING

Some deer began to fly.

They would mostly fly at night.

Some of them did this for a *Lost Boys* vampiric feeling, others for a Ramond Briggs *Snowman*, more wholesome children's story vibe. An elite few were chasing a more high-brow, Roy Andersson, Marc Chagall buzz.

They found evidence on a cave wall that their ancestors had also flown and felt this validated their activity.

Some more irreverent deer decided to go against the grain and to get into swimming and deep-sea diving instead.

No cave drawings depicted *that*, they said to each other, smugly, in deer language.

Sometimes when the swimming deer swam on their backs near the surface of the water looking up at the night sky, they would see the flying deer, if the flying deer were swooping low.

In these moments their eyes would lock, and an upbeat, euphoric, electronic melody would reverberate, whilst an explosive torrent of metallic pink hearts and gold stars zipped around the sky above them.

This meant that they had completed level one and would progress to level two with no further delay.

MOON

Some deer noticed the moon was dripping.
There was moon juice all over the forest.
Perhaps there was a leak, some of the deer suggested to each other in deer language.
But the majority felt the moon juice was spread too far, wide and evenly for it to be that.
The deer started licking the moon juice and not only did it give them special powers (they could recite the script of the film *Labyrinth* backwards as they'd always desired), but it also activated the forest juke box, which had been dusty and dormant for some time.
Songs like, Audrey Hepburn's version of 'Moon River'; 'The Killing Moon' by Echo and the Bunnyman, and 'Man on the Moon' by REM started playing loudly.
So loudly, the deer didn't hear when hunters came to hunt them, and suddenly 'The Killing Moon' took on a whole new meaning.
Survivors struggled to see the funny side of this until many years later.

WAG

Some deer started wagging their tails in the manner of language or morse code.
"Oh we like this!", they said to each other in deer language, communicating through their tails.
The tails were so expressive and there was so much movement and nuance, they decided to make a kid's show out of them, in the same vein as Punch and Judy.
Deer came from miles around to see the production.
The psychological depth explored was astounding, the merchandise reflected but failed to capture in a catchy phrase.
Sadly, the deer who were the top performers decided they couldn't cope with the pressure anymore and wanted to go back to how things were before.
But by then they were contractually bound and forced to honour their agreements.
Many of them developed arthritic tails and a deep depression as the years went by.
They started to despise their tails and wished they'd never wagged them in the first place.
Eventually they did a deal with a slightly dodgy, entrepreneurial Gosshawk, who replaced their tails with wax work models of Henry VIII's wives, a move which created a clever little loop, and they were eventually released from all bonds and obligations.

BLUE

A blue deer arrived and was silent.

Some deer had tried to interrogate the blue deer, to find out its story, where it came from and what it knew. But the blue deer wouldn't crack.

The blue deer was a closed door, they said to each other in deer language.

On day three, the blue deer took a stick and made an arc shape with a cross in the middle and a shape that looked like a bicycle clip in the corner in the ground.

Then it started to do a little hop-based dance and held its face in an expression of pleading for approximately twelve seconds then went back to normal.

Still the deer was closed.

So they set it alight and watched it go up in a puff of blue smoke.

The fumes gave them a very specific feeling, that of a person encountering the work of singer Julio Iglesias or Barry Manilow for the first time during the 1980s.

They were surprisingly sad once the blue deer had turned to ashes and decided to go looking for another one, to no avail.

BLANKED

Some deer started avoiding some of the other deer and those deer were avoiding another group of deer again.

This was no way to live, one of the deer said in deer language, to a bunch of deer it wasn't avoiding.

Maybe not, one replied, but on the island of La Gomera, this is the only way *to* live.

It's a style and an attitude.

They have a publication called *Avoidance Monthly*.

And an accompanying game show.

You can win quite a lot of browse, forbs, mast and grass, apparently.

The deer who heard this turned into blades of grass.

The deer gods, treating them as reeds, held them between their hooves and whistled.

TREE

Some deer noticed that one of the trees in the forest started growing small parcels.
They were immaculately wrapped and "more like gifts, really", they all established in deer language.
They started pulling off the ones they could reach with their teeth and unwrapping them with their teeth also.
(Yes, there was a knack to this.)
They were not amused to find that Black Jacks and fake blood capsules were inside the packages.
Mostly as they had the forest photographer coming that day and they would now look like demons in the picture for the *Forest Gazette*.

RUT

Some deer were nervous more than excited about the upcoming rutting period.

Last year had been a bit of a disaster.

Under a rutting spell some of the deer had run on the road at the edge of the forest searching for more rutting action.

Problem was, a Robin Reliant that was time travelling from the 1970s came along at that exact time, accidently impaled one of the deer, and took them back to the 1970s.

None of the deer had time to warn whoever was driving that that particular deer had an aversion to *Saturday Night Fever*, so if they survived, it would be in everyone's interest to keep it away from said film, and disco in general.

The potential consequences were unspeakable, they agreed in deer language, but the deer died en route, so turned out it was a load of worrying about nothing.

PRIEST

Some deer were blessed by a priest.
This meant the deer could immediately carry out wrong doings and they were covered.
Other deer were jealous and went to get blessed also.
Pretty soon everyone was blessed and carrying out wrong doings.
They locked up the priest so that he would have to bless them whenever their blessing ran out. On average it was about twenty-five days.
The priest was having regrets but being locked away kept him out of trouble at least.
The conditions that he was living in were better than the psychiatric ward at the prison from which he escaped, and the deer never found that he wasn't really a priest.

GRAVEL

Some deer walked over gravel.

They enjoyed the sound so much that they walked over gravel again.

They also enjoyed the sensation, so a portion of them decided that this is what they would like to dedicate the rest of their lives to now.

Some other deer didn't get it, so splinter groups were formed.

There was much criticism of the deer for liking such a dull activity, but others said that if it made them happy, why not.

What was really creeping them out, the other deer said, in deer language, was that the deer on the gravel had started smiling.

Deer didn't smile, the other deer scowled.

The scowling deer were then mocked by some local geese for their glowers.

Consequently, they gave in and indulged in the gravel walking.

Within hours their faces became set in a kind of smirk.

From their smirks a grotesque pantomime began, which ran for forever.

ACKNOWLEDGEMENTS

Thanks to *Gutter: New Scottish and International Writing* for publishing 'Windscreens' and 'Tuxedo'.

Thanks to Kristofor Minta for telling me all about his experiences living with the overpopulation of deer in Syracuse and getting me thinking about and visualising deer back in March, 2023. Thanks also to Leslie Minnis for her gorgeous double-doe design on Chelsea Minnis's *Zirconia...Bad Bad* published by Fence (2019), which I had tattooed on my arm in January 2023. These two factors are how and why *Some Deer* came into being!

Thanks to POG group in Edinburgh for discussing some of these poems with me.

Thanks to my partner Nicky Melville for additional dee[a]r discussions along the way.

LAY OUT YOUR UNREST

www.ingramcontent.com/pod-product-compliance
Lightning Source LLC
Chambersburg PA
CBHW051741040426
42447CB00008B/1246